Spiritual Ink

JOURNAL

WRITING PROMPTS TO SPARK YOUR SOUL

SHANNON ALFORD

Book Design & Production:
Columbus Publishing Lab
www.ColumbusPublishingLab.com

Copyright © 2024 by Shannon Alford

All rights reserved.
This book, or parts thereof, may not be
reproduced in any form without permission.

Paperback ISBN: 978-1-63337-911-4

Printed in the United States of America
1 3 5 7 9 10 8 6 4 2

Dedication

To my husband, Ed, and my daughter, Audrey,
the people who most spark my soul

AND

TO THE TEAM OF COUSINS:

Alexa
Audrey
Austin
Abby
Nick

You were loved and prayed for long before you were born into our family.
You are each extraordinary and you have a special bond between you.
The days are bright before you!

Suggested companion guide from the author

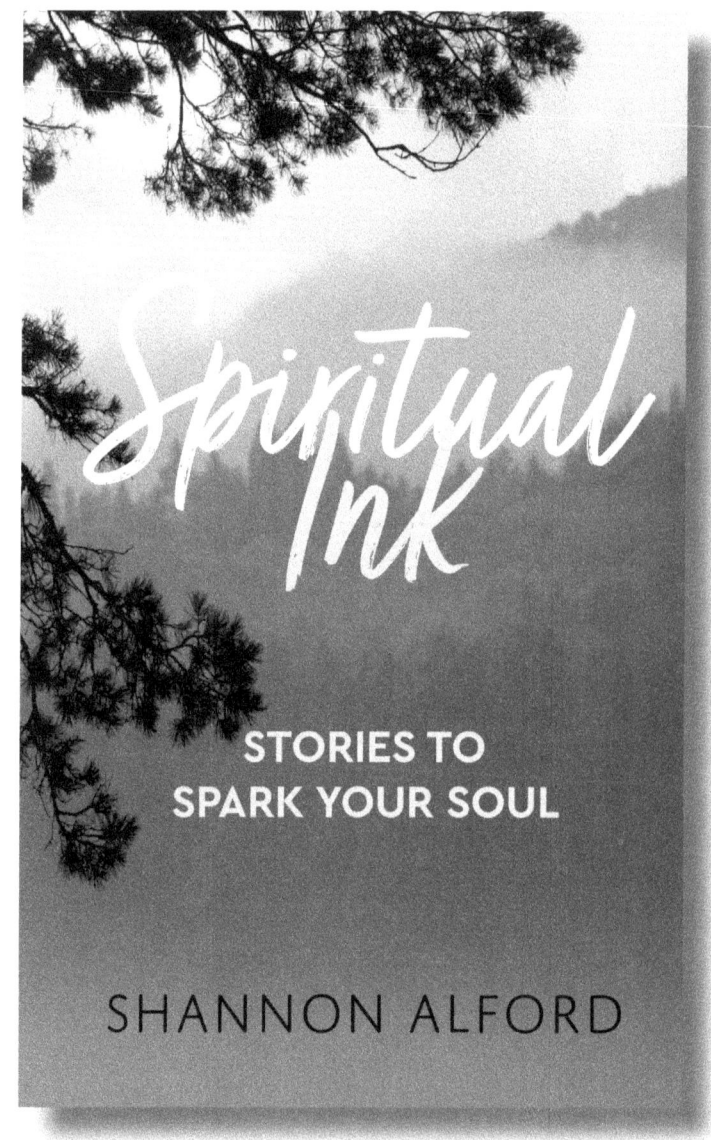

Available worldwide wherever you buy your books!

Introduction

There are deeper levels of creativity within you and journaling is a way to become more attuned to your thoughts and emotions. Our bodies are embedded with wisdom and we perceive more information than we realize. Sometimes it takes awhile for information to sift through our consciousness. The pace of life is really fast and taking time to quiet your mind and body to sit down and write or type out your thoughts encourages creative thought and flexibility in thinking.

Ideas generate even more ideas as you engage your imagination and broaden your perspective to notice things that maybe you haven't noticed before. Reflective writing can help you ponder your experiences, process difficult emotions, and deepen your intuition.

I began journaling years ago after I started working the evening shift in a busy pediatric emergency department as a Child Life Specialist helping children cope with the stress of hospitalization and medical intervention. The work was challenging and rewarding but at night I experienced restless sleep and bad dreams from the number of interactions I encountered on a daily basis and the intensity of the situations that flooded into the emergency department continually.

I began to write about some of the conversations that were meaningful to me and it helped me to think about what I had seen or learned. I also began to use quotes or pieces of conversations as writing prompts. I noticed that reflecting on my interactions and those of others around me helped strengthen my clinical skills and the practice of pouring out my thoughts on paper about anything and everything was its own reward. My stress level and anxiety decreased and my sleep improved.

Once I began writing, I remembered a course I had taken in college on death and dying which was a semester of writing assignments and journaling any dreams recalled from the night before. The small group discussions were dynamic and the other students, like me, were introduced to thinking about issues pertaining to life, death, and eternity that we hadn't considered before.

Just as children leave play experiences more content and peaceful than when they began, writing does the same for me. Then and now, I journal sporadically because it works best for me but a friend of mine journals every day. It's a matter of personal preference but journaling contributed to the longevity and enjoyment of hospital work for many years before I left to pursue other interests.

During that time I worked with different patient populations including the cardiology unit and intensive care. I had the opportunity to offer journaling supplies and activities for creative expression to children, adolescents, and adults and it was embraced more enthusiastically than I could have anticipated. I think it's because writing helps us become more introspective and additionally, our imagination invites us beyond the limitations of a physical location.

We are both physical and spiritual in nature and when we are more present in the moment, we feel more positive and appreciative of the life we've been given. As we communicate with others, both verbally and nonverbally, on our journey through life, each interaction leaves an etch on our human hearts which I refer to as "Spiritual Ink."

Whether you are new to journaling or have been writing out your thoughts for some time, I hope you find this resource beneficial and enjoyable.

- The left page of the journal is for you to use however you want—to use different pens, colored pencils, draw, glue or tape photos or magazine pages. You are the artist and the audience.

- Date your entries.

- Write a short or long amount, whatever is on your mind. You can use the writing prompts, which are only suggestions, or create your own.

- Pay attention to any recurring themes, ideas, or messages in your writing and your dreams and any clues you decipher from it.

- If the subject matter is personal or sensitive, consider writing it out on notebook paper and throwing it away afterwards.

- Keep Post-it notes nearby to write down any distracting thoughts, like phone calls or emails to return, so you can return your attention back to your writing.

- Be nonjudgmental in your attitude and have fun!

It is sown a natural body, it is raised a spiritual body,
If there is a natural body, there is also a spiritual body.

1 Corinthians 15:44 (NIV)

....

You show that you are a letter from Christ, the result of our ministry,
written not with ink but with the Spirit of the living God,
not on tablets of stone but on tablets of human hearts.

2 Corinthians 3:3 (NIV)

Dream Journal

Dream Journal

Dream Journal

Dream Journal

Dream Journal

Journal 1

Date: _____

Write about one of your friends and the friendship between you. How did you meet and what are the dynamics of your relationship? Journal about something you have learned together or from one another.

_____
_____
_____
_____
_____
_____
_____
_____
_____
_____
_____
_____
_____
_____
_____
_____
_____
_____
_____
_____
_____
_____
_____
_____
_____

Journal 2

Date:_____

Write about a pet or an animal that makes you happy or has brought meaning to your life.

_____
_____
_____
_____
_____
_____
_____
_____
_____
_____
_____
_____
_____
_____
_____
_____
_____
_____
_____
_____
_____
_____
_____
_____

Journal 3

Date: _____

Who is someone who inspires you and why? What similarities and differences do you share with them?

_____
_____
_____
_____
_____
_____
_____
_____
_____
_____
_____
_____
_____
_____
_____
_____
_____
_____
_____
_____
_____
_____
_____
_____
_____
_____

Journal 4

Date: _____

Write about anything that makes you laugh.

Journal 5

Date: _____

What song, book, quote, or scripture feels especially meaningful to you right now and why?

_____
_____
_____
_____
_____
_____
_____
_____
_____
_____
_____
_____
_____
_____
_____
_____
_____
_____
_____
_____
_____
_____
_____
_____
_____

Journal 6

Date: _____

Write about some happy memories from a vacation you took. Where did you go and who were you with? What were some of the highlights? Would you like to visit there again or would you prefer to explore new destinations?

_____
_____
_____
_____
_____
_____
_____
_____
_____
_____
_____
_____
_____
_____
_____
_____
_____
_____
_____
_____
_____
_____
_____
_____

Journal 7

Date: _____

Write about a time you encouraged someone going through a difficult time or when someone encouraged you. What was done or said to contribute positivity and support?

Journal 8

Date: _____

What do you do for fun and how do you spend your free time?

Journal 9

Date: _____

Journal about a situation you were worried about in the past. How did it get resolved and would you handle the situation differently from your perspective now?

_____
_____
_____
_____
_____
_____
_____
_____
_____
_____
_____
_____
_____
_____
_____
_____
_____
_____
_____
_____
_____
_____
_____
_____

Journal 10

Date: _____

Is there a cause or organization you use your time, talent, or financial support to contribute to? If not, is there one you would like to donate to in some way in the future?

_____
_____
_____
_____
_____
_____
_____
_____
_____
_____
_____
_____
_____
_____
_____
_____
_____
_____
_____
_____
_____
_____
_____
_____

Journal 11

Date:_____

What is one of your favorite foods and when was the last time you had it? Where were you and who were you with?

_____
_____
_____
_____
_____
_____
_____
_____
_____
_____
_____
_____
_____
_____
_____
_____
_____
_____
_____
_____
_____
_____
_____

Journal 12

Date: _____

Write about a time you experienced coincidences as a sign of God's divine intervention and direction and how things worked together for your benefit.

_____
_____
_____
_____
_____
_____
_____
_____
_____
_____
_____
_____
_____
_____
_____
_____
_____
_____
_____
_____
_____
_____
_____
_____
_____

Journal 13

Date: _____

Write about an area of growth or self-improvement you've made progress in.

_____
_____
_____
_____
_____
_____
_____
_____
_____
_____
_____
_____
_____
_____
_____
_____
_____
_____
_____
_____
_____
_____
_____
_____
_____

Journal 14

Date: _____

When you were a child, were there interests or activities you enjoyed that helped direct you towards a career or volunteer involvement?

_____
_____
_____
_____
_____
_____
_____
_____
_____
_____
_____
_____
_____
_____
_____
_____
_____
_____
_____
_____
_____
_____
_____
_____

Journal 15

Date: _____

What are two or three of your personality traits or strengths that you appreciate about yourself?

_____
_____
_____
_____
_____
_____
_____
_____
_____
_____
_____
_____
_____
_____
_____
_____
_____
_____
_____
_____
_____
_____
_____
_____
_____
_____

Journal 16

Date: _____

Write about a time you worked well within a group setting such as a sports team, classroom, or at work.

Journal 17

Date: _____

Can you be honest with God about the matters in your heart and mind? If not, what do you think is holding you back?

_____
_____
_____
_____
_____
_____
_____
_____
_____
_____
_____
_____
_____
_____
_____
_____
_____
_____
_____
_____
_____
_____
_____
_____
_____

# Journal 18

Date: _____

What are some ways you can be a better friend to yourself?

Journal 19

Date: _____

Write about a time you made a mistake by something you said or did. How did you grow from it? From your current perspective, what would you have done differently if you were able to repeat it?

Journal 20

Date: _____

Do you play an instrument or is there one you would like to learn to play?

Journal 21

Date: _____

Do you have good friends you can trust or do you think you might need to make some changes concerning the people, environments, or entertainment choices influencing you?

_____
_____
_____
_____
_____
_____
_____
_____
_____
_____
_____
_____
_____
_____
_____
_____
_____
_____
_____
_____
_____
_____
_____
_____

Journal 22

Date: _____

Is there anyone or anything you feel especially called to pray for right now?

Journal 23

Date: _____

Describe an area in your home that especially brings you joy or contentment. Consider what things contribute to making it so comfortable such as photos, plants, furniture, paint color, or candles.

Journal 24

Date: _____

Is there someone you need to forgive? How would it feel to be free from that burden even if they were in the wrong? Could you work towards praying for them and releasing them into God's hands to deal with and to release you from its hold?

_____
_____
_____
_____
_____
_____
_____
_____
_____
_____
_____
_____
_____
_____
_____
_____
_____
_____
_____
_____
_____
_____
_____

Journal 25

Date: _____

Have you ever encountered a health crisis? What helped you through? Do you have any advice you would share with someone else facing illness or medical intervention?

Journal 26

Date: _____

What are some ways you can foster creative thought and artistic expression in your life right now? What are things you enjoy such as cooking, gardening, photography, or painting?

_____
_____
_____
_____
_____
_____
_____
_____
_____
_____
_____
_____
_____
_____
_____
_____
_____
_____
_____
_____
_____
_____
_____

Journal 27

Date: _____

Have you experienced conflict with a friend or a coworker that ultimately resulted in a more respectful or closer relationship afterwards? Write about it.

Journal 28

Date:_____

When was the last time you laughed and what was it about?

Journal 29

Date: _____

Write about a time recently when you were outside in nature and some of the things you noticed that activated your senses.

_____
_____
_____
_____
_____
_____
_____
_____
_____
_____
_____
_____
_____
_____
_____
_____
_____
_____
_____
_____
_____
_____
_____
_____

Journal 30

Date: _____

What are some dreams and aspirations you have for the future?

Conclusion

Congratulations on working through the Spiritual Ink Journal! Thank you for your participation and I hope these writing exercises have been beneficial for you.

What was your experience with journaling through these pages? Was it useful to you and did you learn anything about yourself in the process? Do you plan to continue journaling?

If it interests you, read a few articles about the practice of reflective writing and compare it with your personal experiences.

May God bless the work of your hands and may you find great purpose in both today and the days to come.

Suggested companion guide from the author

Available worldwide wherever you buy your books!

About the Author

Shannon Alford writes to encourage others through her humor, inspiration, and faith. She is a Child Life Specialist with over twenty years of experience working at a pediatric hospital helping children and families struggling with trauma, illness, and loss. She loves writing, encouraging others in their creative pursuits, and spending time with her family and two rescue dogs.

www.ingramcontent.com/pod-product-compliance
Lightning Source LLC
Chambersburg PA
CBHW040009080526
44586CB00028B/2936